Orthotists & Prosthetists

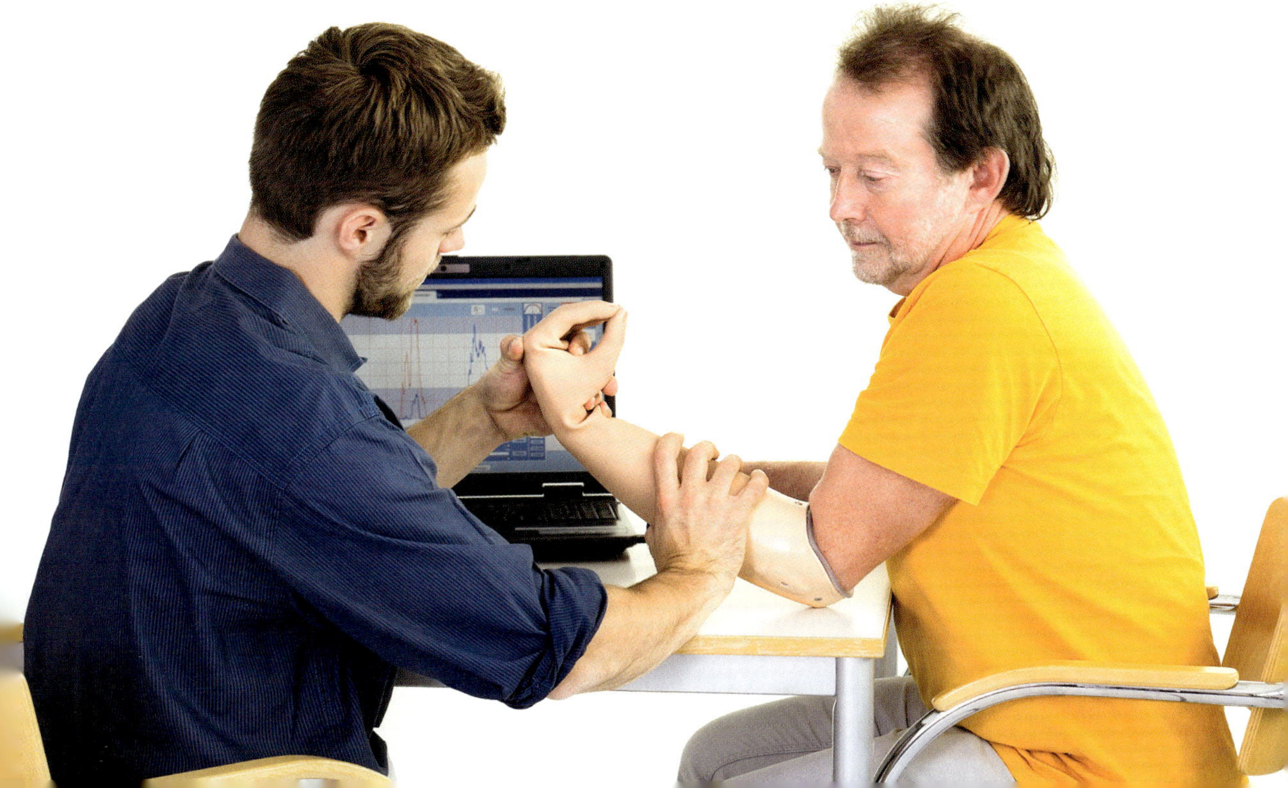

Careers in Healthcare

Athletic Trainers
Clinical & Medical Laboratory Scientists
Dental Hygienists
Dietitian Nutritionists
EMTs & Paramedics
Nurses
Occupational Therapists
Orthotists & Prosthetists
Physical Therapists
Physician Assistants
Respiratory Therapists
Speech Pathologists & Audiologists
Ultrasound Technicians

Orthotists & Prosthetists

Samantha Simon

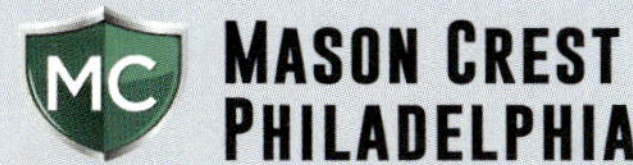
MASON CREST
PHILADELPHIA

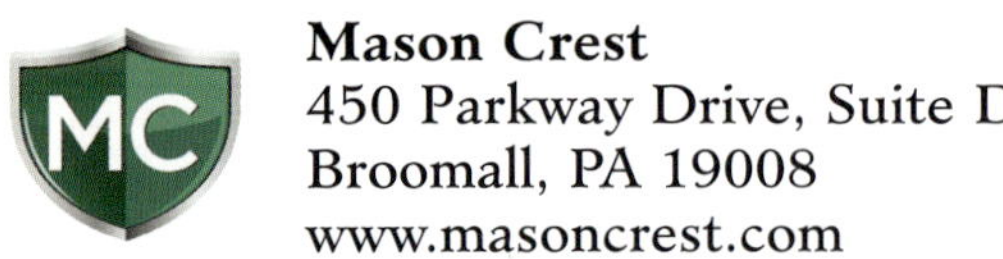

Mason Crest
450 Parkway Drive, Suite D
Broomall, PA 19008
www.masoncrest.com

Printed and bound in the United States of America.

CPSIA Compliance Information: Batch #CHC2017.
For further information, contact Mason Crest at 1-866-MCP-Book.

First printing
1 3 5 7 9 8 6 4 2

Library of Congress Cataloging-in-Publication Data

on file at the Library of Congress
ISBN: 978-1-4222-3802-8 (hc)
ISBN: 978-1-4222-7990-8 (ebook)

Careers in Healthcare series ISBN: 978-1-4222-3794-6

QR CODES AND LINKS TO THIRD-PARTY CONTENT

Table of Contents

KEY ICONS TO LOOK FOR:

Words to understand: These words with their easy-to-understand definitions will increase the reader's understanding of the text while building vocabulary skills.

Sidebars: This boxed material within the main text allows readers to build knowledge, gain insights, explore possibilities, and broaden their perspectives by weaving together additional information to provide realistic and holistic perspectives.

Educational Videos: Readers can view videos by scanning our QR codes, providing them with additional educational content to supplement the text. Examples include news coverage, moments in history, speeches, iconic sports moments and much more!

Text-dependent questions: These questions send the reader back to the text for more careful attention to the evidence presented there.

Research projects: Readers are pointed toward areas of further inquiry connected to each chapter. Suggestions are provided for projects that encourage deeper research and analysis.

Series glossary of key terms: This back-of-the book glossary contains terminology used throughout this series. Words found here increase the reader's ability to read and comprehend higher-level books and articles in this field.

Prosthetics try to bring people back to their full potential, even giving them the ability to run or play sports again.

Words to Understand in This Chapter

amputation—the process of surgically removing a limb or another body part.

baby-boomer population—the post–World War II generation, born in the United States between 1945 and 1964; during this time there was a higher-than-average birth rate.

bilateral amputee—an amputee who has had both limbs removed, either both arms or both legs.

biomechanics—the understanding of movement and the workings of living things, specifically humans.

orthotics—the making of artificial joints, splints, and braces.

prosthesis—an artificial limb or other body part.

prosthetics—the making and fitting of artificial limbs or other body parts.

1

What Is a Prosthetist or Orthotist?

Medicine and technology are constantly intertwining to make human life better. A perfect example of this is the field of ***prosthetics***. A ***prosthesis*** is an artificial body part, usually placed in or on the human body to allow for normal movement or function. People lose limbs or suffer orthopedic impairment for many reasons, including accidents, combat injuries, birth defects, and debilitating diseases. Patients may also need orthopedic braces, also known as orthoses. The health care workers who specialize in these artificial limbs are called orthotists and prosthetists. O&Ps, the shorthand term, help their patients regain their mobility by fitting them with artificial limbs and braces.

The duties of orthotists and prosthetists include:

- Performing a detailed assessment to determine the patient's *orthotic* or prosthetic needs.
- Assessing the patient's status, including her mobility, muscle strength, sensory function, range of motion, and joint stability to allow for the best prosthesis or brace.
- Developing a plan that addresses the patient's needs and goals.
- Selecting the appropriate design, materials, and components for optimum strength, durability, and function.
- Measuring and fitting the proper artificial body part, joint, splint, or brace for the patient.
- Discussing treatment plans with the patient.
- Training the patient in the proper use of the prosthetic or orthotic device.
- Creating the device and making adjustments for proper alignment, maximum function, and comfort.
- Explaining how to maintain the device; this is crucial for the patient because the device is now part of her body.
- Providing follow-up care with patients and help with any needs they have with their devices.

Orthotists and prosthetists may work in both orthotics and prosthetics, or they may specialize in working with a particular area or population. Orthotists are specifically trained to work with medical support devices, such as spinal or knee braces, also known as orthoses. Prosthetists are specifically trained to work with prostheses, such as artificial limbs and other body parts.

Prosthetists

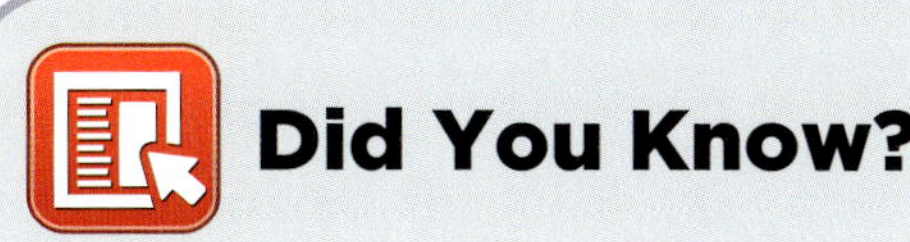

The word *prosthetic* is Greek for "addition."

Prosthetists are health care professionals who evaluate, create, and custom-fit artificial limbs, known as prostheses. Prostheses are used to enhance the function and lifestyle of people with limb loss. Prosthetic patients may have been born with limb deficiency or have experienced ***amputation*** due to trauma, cancer or other life-threatening diseases, infection, or abnormalities in blood vessels or nerves that required amputations. The prosthesis is custom-made for each patient and must be a unique combination of appropriate materials, alignment, design, and construction. These prostheses, which are machines and enhancements to replicate limbs, allow for greater movement and function for patients and give them a better quality of life.

Orthotists

Orthotists are medical professionals who make, fit, and adjust different types of orthopedic braces, known as orthoses. Orthotists draw on their knowledge of anatomy, physiology, ***biomechanics***, and engineering. Orthoses are external braces and devices that are used to modify the structural and functional characteristics of the neuromuscular and skeletal system. These braces allow for better movement, aid in rehabilitation, correct shapes of bones or parts of

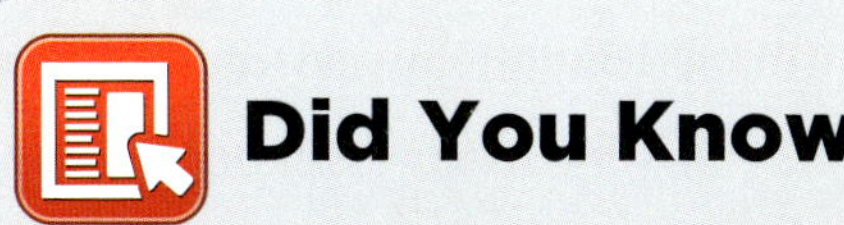

One out of every 200 people in the United States has undergone an amputation.

the body, and even enable people requiring these orthoses to play sports.

A Team Approach

Some orthotists and prosthetists construct individualized custom-made devices for their patients. Medical appliance technicians supervise the construction of the orthotic or prosthetic devices. All the health care professionals who are treating the patient, including therapists, doctors, and nurses, work hand in hand on teams for patients with prostheses and orthoses.

This fascinating field encompasses a variety of specialized careers, each of which contributes to designing, making, fitting, modifying, repairing, and maintaining orthotic and prosthetic devices. In addition to creating these limbs, prosthetists and orthotists focus on assisting patients in using them correctly, fitting them to their body, and making them responsive to the patients' specific needs.

Prosthetists make various types of prosthetics for all sorts of patients, male and female.

Knee braces are one of the most common braces made by orthotists for athletes.

No orthotics or prosthetics are the same. It is all dependent on the patient's needs.

“An Experience I’ll Never Forget”

A prosthetist was asked to share a real-life story about an experience he had had with a patient that would stay with him forever. He responded:

> There was a person who was in the armed services and made it through two tours in Iraq, and when he came back he got hit by a drunk driver and became a ***bilateral amputee***, losing both legs. That still sticks in my mind, but you have to keep a positive attitude with it. I created the prostheses for this person and was able to see him improve. It was amazing seeing a bilateral amputee go from being in a wheelchair to walking on his own again. I am extremely fortunate to be able to help a person who has put his life on the line to fight for this country and ultimately get his function back. I am honored to serve him.

Job Outlook

Employment opportunities for orthotists and prosthetists are projected to grow 23 percent from 2014 to 2024. This is almost two times faster than the average for all occupations, and one of the highest percentages in the medical field. The only downside is that this profession is extremely small. So only about 1,900 new jobs will be created over that ten-year period. This amounts to many fewer jobs in comparison to other health care

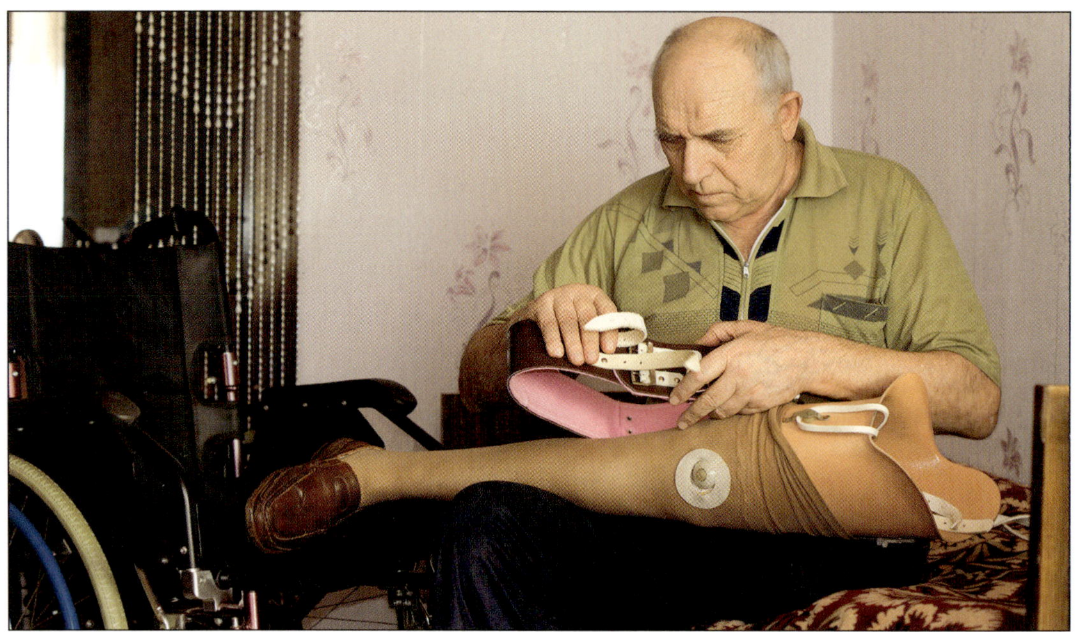

Prosthetics and orthotics are growing in demand, in part due to the aging population.

professions, such as nursing, which is creating tens of thousands of jobs.

The projected surge in jobs in the prosthetist-orthotist profession stems from the large ***baby-boomer population***. This aging population will create an increasing need for orthotists and prosthetists because limb loss is most commonly seen among the geriatric population. Why? Because diabetes and cardiovascular disease, both prevalent among seniors, are the leading causes of limb loss. In addition, people are living longer as a result of advancements in medicine and technology. As a result, these older people will continue to need devices designed and fitted by orthotists and prosthetists, such as braces and orthopedic footwear, to help with movement and stability as they enter old age.

Advancements in technology and medicine are also enabling people to survive traumatic events and accidents that were previously fatal. Improvements in emergency medicine have boosted the survival rates from accidents and traumatic events exponentially. Patients with traumatic injuries, such as combat veterans, will also continue to need orthotists and prosthetists. This creates even greater demand for those in the prosthetist-orthotist professions.

Text-Dependent Questions

1. What do prosthetists make? What do orthotists make?
2. What are the two diseases that cause most limb loss?
3. What are three causes of limb loss that may prompt a need for prostheses?

Research Project

Look up two different types of prostheses and two different types of orthoses and figure out what they are used for.

Most prosthetics are either made for injured war veterans or for people who have had a limb amputated due to disease.

Words to Understand in This Chapter

osteoarthritis—the degeneration of joint cartilage and the underlying bone within the body, causing very brittle bones and pain.

osteoporosis—the disease in which the bones become brittle and fragile from loss of tissue over time.

plaster modification—the shaping and molding of plaster to make orthoses or prostheses.

three-dimensional printer—a printer that prints in three dimensions by layering different materials on top of each other to create certain objects.

vascular disease—any disease dealing with blood flow to limbs or parts of the body; specifically, diseases dealing with arteries or veins throughout the body.

2

A Look at the Opportunities

Approximately 185,000 amputations occur in the United States each year. Employment of orthotists and prosthetists is projected to grow 23 percent from 2014 to 2024. This projection makes the prosthetist-orthotist profession one of the fastest-growing fields, in relation to all careers, and one of the fastest-growing within the health care field.

These professionals are finding increasing opportunities because the baby-boomer generation is getting older and living longer. This baby-boomer population is not only large in number, but living much longer than previous generations, prompting a surge in demand for braces and prostheses. Prostheses and orthoses are needed for these baby boomers because of their high rate of *osteoporosis*, *osteoarthritis*, and the long-term

"An Experience I'll Never Forget"

A prosthetist was asked to explain what inspired him to to get into this field of work. He responded:

> I worked in a rehab setting before, and I did work with some people who had undergone amputations. I really liked the people, and was fascinated with the mechanics and how prostheses worked with them. It was a nice combination of art and science—from using your hands to make the socket to aligning and programming any type of microprocessor. And on top of that, you get to spend a lot of time with the people and really get to know them, as opposed to just treating the diagnosis.

wear and tear on their aging bones and joints. Another reason there is such a demand for these prostheses is the high rate of diabetes and cardiovascular disease among this population. The main cause of limb loss is ***vascular disease***, which includes diabetes and peripheral arterial disease; roughly 54 percent of limb loss is caused by these two diseases alone. In addition, as a result of advances in emergency medicine, the survival rates for accidents and traumas have grown exponentially. Patients with traumatic injuries, such as combat veterans or accident victims, will also continue to need orthotists and prosthetists.

The new technology of ***three-dimensional printers*** has made the design and manufacture of prostheses and orthoses more precise and cutting edge. This allows for blueprints to more accurately reflect the patient's measurements and his specific needs, and reduces error in creating the artificial limbs.

To understand the career of prosthetists or orthotists, you must understand how their time is divided. They split their time between working with patients in an office or clinic setting, and building devices in a laboratory or workshop.

The first step in an orthotist's or prosthetist's job is to evaluate the patient—not just the injury, but the patient as well. During this evaluation, the prosthetist or orthotist seeks to get a full understanding of the patient, and what that person's goals are. In addition, the prosthetist or orthotist takes key measurements to begin the process of creating the prosthesis or orthosis.

From there, the prosthetist or orthotist goes back to his workshop and starts to make molds of the model. This model is then fitted and adjusted for functionality on the patient. The final prosthesis or orthosis is then made, and the patient is trained in how to use it.

At this point, it is common for prosthetists-orthotists to work closely with other medical professionals, including doctors, nurses, orthopedic surgeons, podiatrists, physical therapists, and occupational therapists to help the patient return to full function. Once that occurs, the patient is routinely brought back to the clinic or physician's office for checkups, and if the patient has any issues with the prosthe-

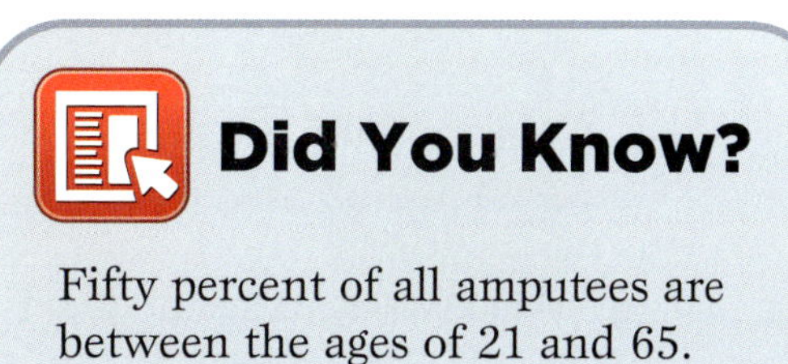

Fifty percent of all amputees are between the ages of 21 and 65.

Many times orthotists or prosthetists have to make house calls to repair damaged prosthetics or braces.

sis or orthosis, the prosthetist or orthotist might have to come in and make adjustments. Other than some occasional after-hour repair calls, prosthetists-orthotists generally work regular business hours, though this may vary depending on the employer.

If you're looking into becoming a prosthetist or orthotist, you must determine if you have the traits needed for this job, including:

Good communication skills: Orthotists and prosthetists must be able to communicate effectively with the technicians who often fabricate the medical devices, and must communicate clearly with other medical professionals working with the patient. They must also be able to explain to patients how to use and care for the devices; this is extremely important because the prosthesis or orthosis becomes part of their body and their very being. Patients use this piece of technology constantly, so they can their improve their movement, their stability, and, ultimately, their life.

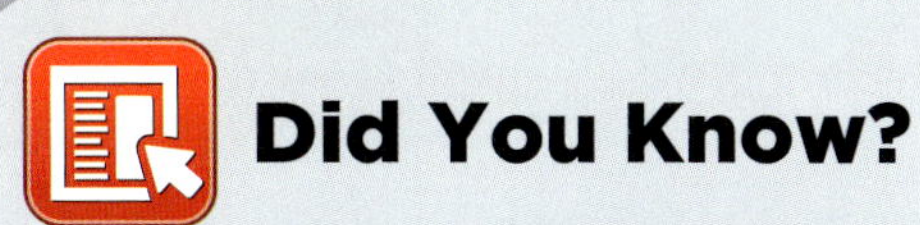

Prostheses are extremely expensive pieces of machinery, costing up to a $100,000 each.

A detail orientation: Orthotists and prosthetists must be very precise in making their orthoses or prostheses. The person designing and creating these prostheses must be extremely detail-oriented, to make sure the prosthesis fits the patient perfectly. From the joint to the digits of the prosthesis, every part is vital in promoting the movement and function of the patient.

Prosthetists have to be extremely detail oriented. All joints or linings that come into contact with the patient's body must be custom fitted to exact measurements.

Patience: Orthotists and prosthetists may work for long periods with patients who need special attention. Also, patients, patients' families, and even technology are not always easy to deal with. Things break at the worst times, and an orthotist or prosthetist must always be understanding and patient. Sometimes prosthetists-orthotists must work the extra hours or come in on weekends to fix people's prostheses or orthoses, to make sure they are in proper working order.

Physical dexterity: Orthotists and prosthetists are constantly working with their hands. They are creating models, using tools, and fitting patients. These medical professionals must be exceedingly good at working with their hands. At any point in

Prosthetists must be skilled at working with tools.

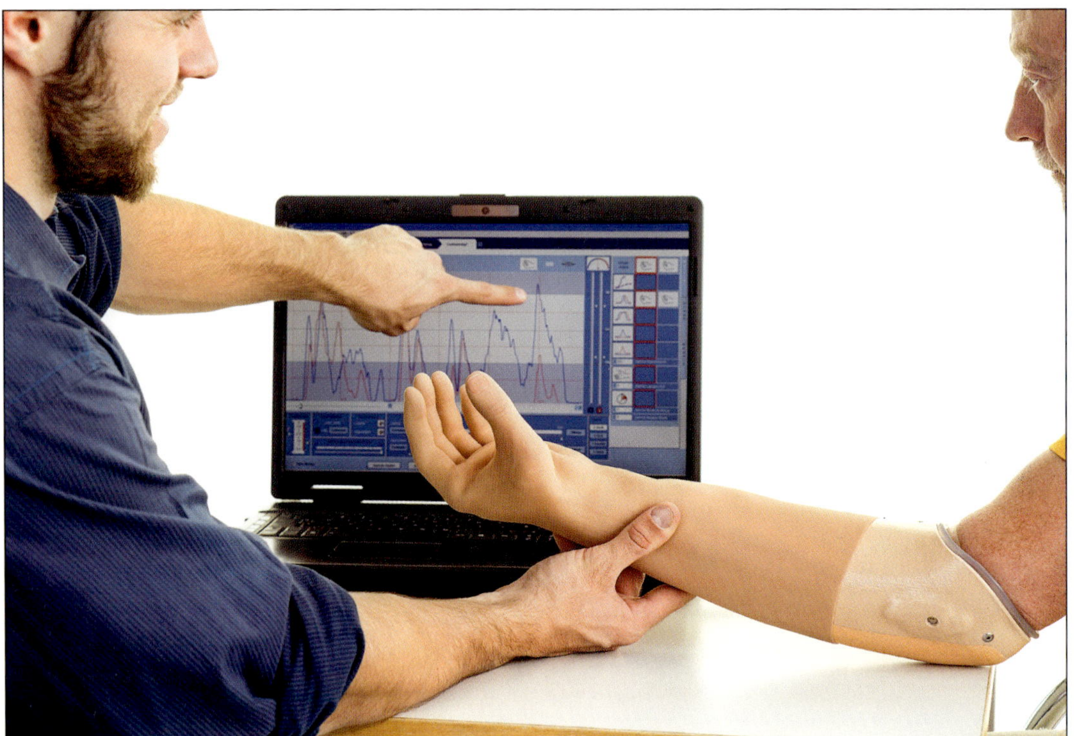

In recent years, there have been many technological advances in the creation of prosthetics and orthotic braces.

the process, they may need to fix the largest of parts or the tiniest of wires, so they must have dexterity when working with these small machines. They primarily use hand tools and shop tools throughout the process, from ***plaster modification*** to joint creation.

Technological savvy: Not only do orthotists and prosthetists use power tools, but they also use computer programs and three-dimensional printers. So these professionals must be tech-savvy. Understanding this technology gives them a leg up in the growing field of biotechnology and medical equipment, and even enables them to pioneer innovations in the field.

Problem-solving skills: Orthotists and prosthetists are constantly solving the problems that are thrown their way. Not only do they have to evaluate their patients' amputation, but their whole-body situation as well. This means they must think creatively and outside the box to find solutions to these problems.

Educational Video

To see a prosthetic technician at work, scan here:

Text-Dependent Questions

1. How many amputations are estimated to occur each year in the United States?
2. What are the typical hours a prosthetist or orthotist works?
3. What are two of the characteristics prosthetists or orthotists should have?

Research Project

Research a local prosthetic or orthotic practice. Look and see what type of prostheses or orthoses they make, what their hours are, what type of setting they have, and any other elements of their work environment.

A bachelor's degree is required to become a prosthetic or orthotic professional.

Words to Understand in This Chapter

CPM exam—the clinical patient management exam, which is the portion of the certification exam for prosthetists and orthotists that tests for patient care and patient management.

extremity—a limb or end of a part of the human body.

kinetics—the study of forces within movements and motion by the human body.

NCOPE—the National Commission on Orthotics and Prosthetics Education, the governing body regulating all education in orthotics and prosthetics.

Education and Training

To become an orthotist or prosthetist, you must complete a four-year undergraduate bachelor's degree, plus a master's degree in orthotics and prosthetics. Beginning in January 2013, the National Commission on Orthotics and Prosthetics Education (*NCOPE*) ruled that a master's degree in orthotics and prosthetics is the minimum educational standard to become a certified practitioner.

Currently there are 13 active master's degree programs in this field in the United States and more are constantly cropping up. To even apply for these programs, you must complete certain prerequisites. These prerequisites usually include biology, chemistry, anatomy, and physiology courses. In the master's programs, future orthotists and prosthetists take classes in upper- and lower-*extremity* orthotics and prosthetics, spinal

While participating in a residency program, students gain hands-on experience manufacturing and fitting prosthetics or orthotics.

orthotics, and plastics and other materials, which future practitioners must be trained in to be able to create and mold machines used for their patients. Students also take courses in higher-level life sciences, anatomy, physiology, ***kinetics***, and biomechanics. In addition, orthotics and prosthetics programs have a clinical component, in which each student works under the direction of an orthotist or prosthetist. This is a sort of residency or internship program.

Following graduation from a master's degree program, candidates must complete a residency that has been accredited by the National Commission on Orthotic and Prosthetic Education. This body accredits and oversees both master's programs and prosthetics and orthotics residencies. These residencies usually last for one year to eighteen months, specifically in orthotics or in prosthetics.

If you want to earn both a prosthetic and an orthotic degree, you must complete a year of residency in prosthetics and a year in orthotics. Alternatively, some master's programs offer a dual residency, which is around eighteen months in length.

One way to get a head start in this educational process is to take preliminary steps in high school. High school students should take higher-level science classes, anatomy courses, physics classes, and even shop classes to understand how to use power tools and basic shop tools. While in high school, students may also find it valuable to take coding or computer programming classes, because prosthetists-orthotists increasingly rely on computer programming and three-dimensional models in making prostheses and orthoses. Computer programming and 3-D modeling are constantly evolving and growing in sophistication, so having a good grounding in these fields will make a big difference as you build your practice.

In addition to completing their residency in orthotics and prosthetics, practitioners must also obtain licensing and certifications.

Certification is required in order to work on any prosthetics or orthotics.

Education Overview

A prosthetist was asked to describe the education and hands-on training that he received before earning a degree in the field. He replied:

> The educational requirements have changed since I became a prosthetist. But my undergraduate degree is in athletic training, then I took a couple of prerequisite classes, based on the path and profession I wanted to go into. Then I went to Northwestern. At that time, the program was just a post-baccalaureate certificate program. This program has actually grown to become a master's program, which requires an additional two years of education and a one-year residency program. So in total you would have about a seven-year program, including the undergraduate program, to have the proper education and training.
>
> Some of the hands-on training I had was when I was an undergrad; we rotated through all the different college sports teams. We worked with them, doing rehabs, injury assessments, and all types of various certified athletic training tasks. The costs in obtaining the degree are similar to any other degree—tuition, books, living costs and any other bills a person might have.

To become a certified prosthetist or orthotist, one must complete a three-part certification exam.

Licensing

Depending on the states where you want to practice as a prosthetist or orthotist, you may or may not need to be licensed. Some states require orthotists and prosthetists to be licensed, while other states only require certification. The states that license orthotists and prosthetists often require certification as a prerequisite to licensing. For the most part, all prosthetists and orthotists get certified: That is the universal requirement to practice in the United States.

Certifications and Examinations

After completing their four years of undergraduate education, plus their master's degree and residency—all at educational institutions with NCOPE-accredited programs—orthotists and prosthetists are then allowed to take the test for certification. This certification is offered by the American Board for Certification in Orthotics, Prosthetics & Pedorthics (ABC) and

Did You Know?

The type of prosthesis a patient needs depends on what part of the limb is missing. There are four types of prostheses: transtibial (when the lower leg is amputated between the ankle and knee), transfemoral (when the leg is amputated above the knee or through the femur), transradial (when the arm is amputated below the elbow), and transhumeral (when the arm is amputated between the elbow and shoulder). In master's programs, future prosthetists and orthotists are trained on how to create and properly fit all four types of prostheses.

the Board of Certification/Accreditation (BOC). This certification involves first completing an application, and then taking a series of three exams. You must pass all three to be allowed to practice. The three exams comprise a written exam, a clinical patient management exam, and a written simulation exam.

Written Exam

The first exam is the main written exam. This written exam is made up of 165 multiple-choice questions that need to be answered in three hours. These questions focus on your knowledge of anatomy, physiology, biomechanics, kinesiology, and disease processes—basically the whole first-year curriculum of the master's program.

Clinical Patient Management (CPM) Exam

The second component is the clinical patient management exam, or *CPM exam*. This exam comprises five hands-on practical assessments of your skills as a direct practitioner. Here you work with a real patient in a real clinical environment. An examiner assesses your interaction with a patient in a clinical environment, plus you respond to two videotaped scenarios in five exam scenarios overall. You must perform specific tasks while demonstrating and describing your orthotic or prosthetic recommendations, fitting criteria, patient instructions, and follow-up plans involved in providing care. This reflects your skills as a prosthetist or orthotist, and especially all you learned in your hands-on training during your residency.

Written Simulation Exam

The third exam is a three-hour, interactive, written exam. This exam is made up of seven simulated case studies and you must provide analysis, patient evaluation, device recommendation, technical implementation, and follow-up protocols. This tests your grasp of clinical problem-solving skills—applying your knowledge of health, anatomy, and other subjects to specific cases.

Text-Dependent Questions

1. How many tests are part of the certification exam to become a certified prosthetist or orthotist?
2. What is the governing body that oversees the accreditation of all prosthetics and orthotics master's programs in the United States?
3. How many total years of schooling, starting in college, are needed to become a certified prosthetist or orthotist today?

Research Project

Look up local master's programs in prosthetics. Find out their tuition per year, their course curriculum, their residency programs, and if they are accredited by NCOPE.

Prosthetics have evolved over time.

Words to Understand in This Chapter

catgut tendons—tough, thin cords, made from the treated and stretched intestines of animals, especially sheep, which are used for stringing musical instruments and tennis rackets and making surgical stitches or sutures.

deformities—misshaped parts of the body, or parts of the body that were not formed normally

patented—referring to an official document stating the right to use an invention or idea.

4

Evolution of the Profession

Before you can examine the history and evolution of the profession of prosthetics or orthotics, you must first dive into the evolution of prostheses. Some of the first-known prostheses were made by early Egyptians around 900 BCE. These were usually made of fiber or wood, and were mainly used to give the person a sense of "wholeness," rather than functionality. That is, they may have been primarily designed to convey the feeling that a person was complete, rather than to help with everyday tasks.

The next advancement in artificial limbs was an artificial leg that dates to 300 BCE in Capua, Italy, but was only discovered in 1858. This artificial leg, made of bronze and iron with a wooden core, was meant for a person who had a below-the-knee amputation. Then, during the Dark Ages (500–1000 CE),

Did You Know?

Scientists recently discovered what is believed to be the world's first prosthetic toe on an Egyptian mummy, and it appears to have been functional.

it was common to see peglegs and hand hooks as artificial limbs. Most of the time, prostheses were used to hide any ***deformities*** or injuries sustained in battle. Yet, unless you were wealthy, you could not afford to get peglegs or hand hooks. Only knights, who were members of the nobility, were fitted for these prostheses at the time; hand hooks and peglegs were not even that functional and were only used to do very basic tasks.

Prosthetists began to emerge at this time. It was common for tradespeople, including armorers, to design and create these artificial limbs. People of all trades often helped make these devices; watchmakers were particularly instrumental in adding intricate internal functions with springs and gears. Many different professionals worked on artificial limbs.

Significant advancements in prosthetics and orthotics began in the early 1500s. In 1508, a German mercenary named Götz von Berlichingen hired a team to make him an advanced pair of iron hands after he lost his right arm in battle. These hands were able to be manipulated and had different settings that conformed with his natural hand. The hand could move by working a series or releases and springs.

During the mid-1500s, a French Army barber/surgeon named Ambroise Paré made great strides in the field of amputation and prosthetics. He is considered by many as the father of modern amputation surgery and prosthetic design. Paré made prostheses for upper- and lower-extremity amputees and created a device for above-the-knee amputation. This device was a kneeling pegleg and foot prosthesis that had a fixed position, an adjustable harness, and knee-lock control. These devices prefigured the prostheses of today. Paré was the first to recognize how a prosthesis should function. A colleague of Paré's named Lorrain, who was a French locksmith, then contributed substantially to the field when he used leather, paper, and glue—in place of heavy iron—to make a prosthesis. This advancement made prostheses lighter and more functional for day-to-day use.

In 1800 a Londoner named James Potts designed a prosthesis made of a wooden shank and socket, a steel knee joint, and an articulated foot that was controlled by ***catgut tendons*** from the knee to the ankle. This became known as the "Anglesey Leg," after the Marquess of Anglesey, who lost his leg in the Battle of Waterloo and wore the leg after the war. A young American then brought the Anglesey leg to the United States in 1839. This man was William Selpho. In the United States, this leg became known as

A Civil War veteran named John W. January shows off the prosthetic legs that were made for him after the war.

Educational Video

To see a video on the future of prosthetics, scan here:

the "Selpho Leg," after Selpho himself.

During the U.S. Civil War (1861–1865), the number of amputations and war injuries reached an all-time high. This forced Americans like James Hanger, a Confederate Army veteran who lost his leg in the war, to start working in the field of prosthetics. As one of the first amputees in the Civil War, Hanger developed the "Hanger Limb."

Benjamin Franklin Palmer of Meredith, New Hampshire, created the first artificial leg ever ***patented*** in the United States. On November 4, 1846, Palmer received a patent for the artificial leg. The artificial leg he created used springs and metal tendons, which allowed for greater range of motion and flexibility in the limb. The springs and tendons acted like joints, allowing for bending and flexibility.

The American Orthotic & Prosthetic Association (AOPA) was founded in 1917 in Washington D.C., as the Artificial

Did You Know?

Contemporary materials, like advanced plastics and carbon-fiber composites, have made prostheses lighter, allowing for greater movement and function for prosthetic patients.

This World War I veteran is using a prosthetic arm to work as a carpenter in a workshop.

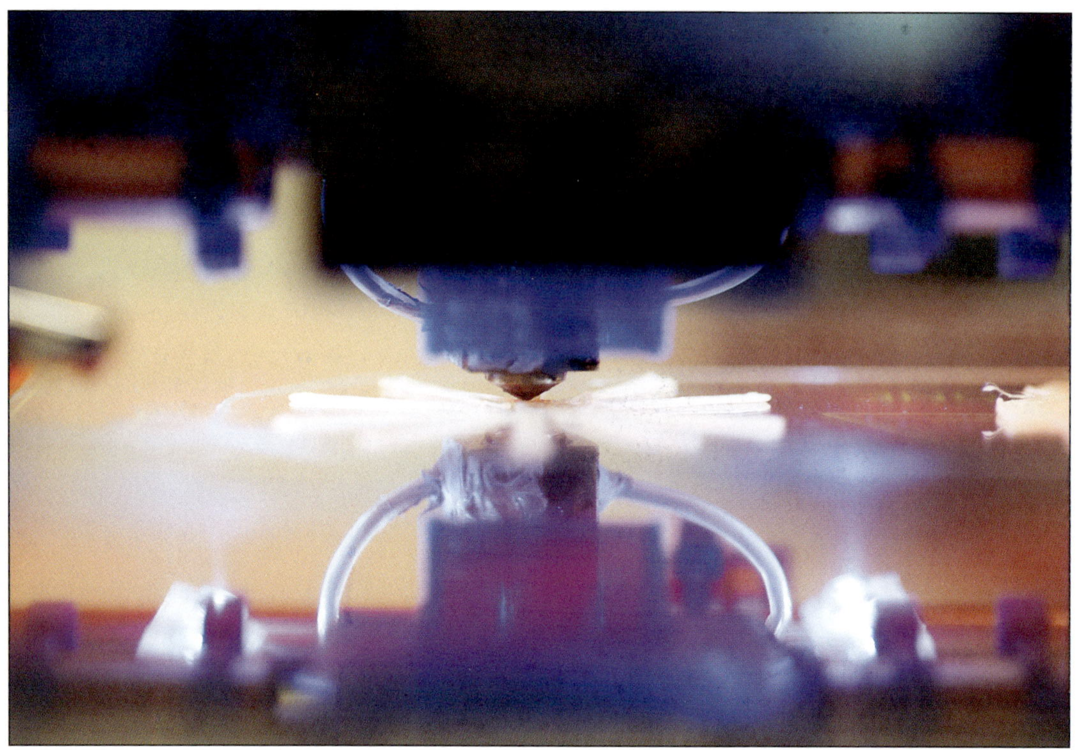

Three-dimensional printers are an important innovation in the creation of modern prosthetics and orthotic braces.

Limb Manufacturers and Brace Association (ALMBA). This was one of the first groups of prosthetists or orthotists in the United States. These professionals were anticipating World War I casualties and knew these soldiers would require orthotic and prosthetic treatment. Because of that, the Council of National Defense and a group of artificial limb and brace manufacturers met to prepare to meet those needs. This was the first organization of brace and prosthetic makers in the United States. This group then evolved into the AOPA, which is the main voice for the orthotics and prosthetics industry today.

Through the years, refinements in mechanisms and materials have kept improving prostheses and orthoses. Yet there is a constant need for advancement in this field. This is the driving force behind the field of orthotics and prosthetics. Most recently, the invention of the three-dimensional printer and targeted computer programming have made the development of artificial limbs and joints much more sophisticated. All professionals in the world of prosthetics and orthotics are working tirelessly to improve artificial limbs and braces.

Text-Dependent Questions

1. What war created a need for a large number of prostheses in the United States?
2. Who patented the first artificial leg in the United States?
3. In what country was the first sign of prostheses seen?

Research Project

Research the first artificial arm and hand. See how that limb has evolved today, and what strides have been made in the field of prosthetic arms and hands.

One of the main goals of prosthetist or orthotists is to get patients back to their full potential, fulfilling the goals they want to achieve.

Words to Understand in This Chapter

fabricate—to create from scratch.

"turn and burn" practices—prosthetics practices that mass-produce prostheses for patients.

5

Overview and Interview

More than 35 million people around the world have disabling conditions that require either an orthosis or prosthesis. This also means 35 million people worldwide are not able to complete all normal life activities because of these impairments. These people are helped by the medical professionals in the prosthetics and orthotics field. From the first-known prosthesis, dating back to ancient Egyptian times, to the three-dimensional printed prostheses of today, the prosthetics and orthotics field has grown with advancements in technology and materials throughout history.

Prosthetists and orthotists *fabricate* and custom-fit artificial limbs and orthopedic braces and other orthoses. On a day-to-day basis, these professionals examine and perform comprehensive assessments of patients. In making these assessments,

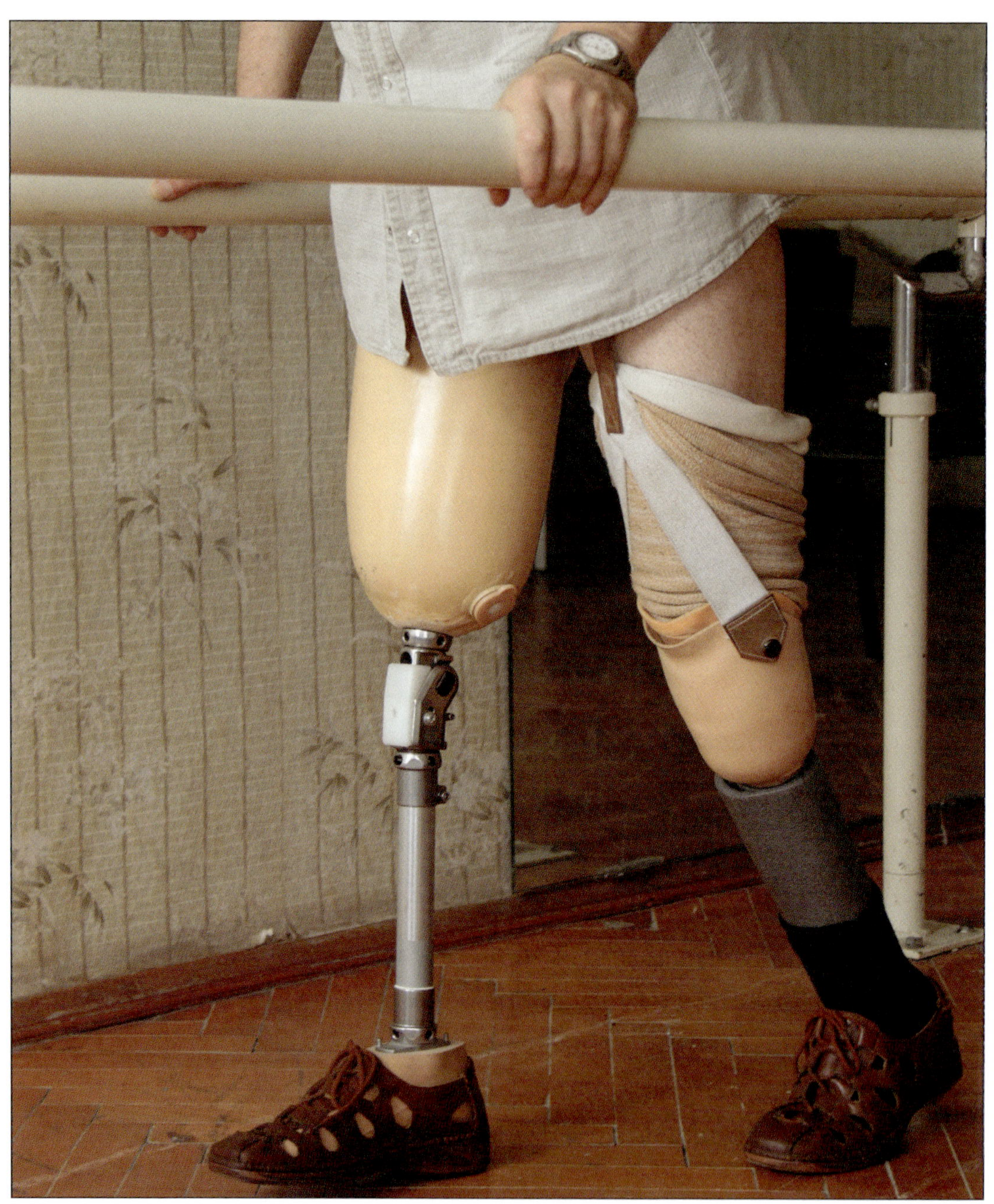

Modern materials have allowed the creation of prostheses that are more flexible and provide greater range of movement for patients.

prosthetists and orthotists determine the patient's needs in terms of orthotics or prosthetics, as well as the patient's goals and previous abilities, prior to the amputation or injury. Then they formulate a treatment plan and a possible prosthetic model. The treatment plan encompasses all fittings and the molding of the prosthesis or orthosis.

They then start creating the prosthesis or orthosis, and adjusting it for the patient, striving for comfort, functionality, flexibility, and overall ease of use by the patient. Implementation of the treatment plan may take from two to five fittings and adjustments, depending on the patient and the intricacy of the artificial limb. Once the limb is fitted, follow-ups are generally required. This means providing continuing patient care and reevaluations to ensure and maintain optimal fit and function of the prosthesis or orthosis. Also, prosthetists or orthotists must also be available at any point to repair any damage done to the prosthesis or orthosis. This may be anywhere from a week after final fitting to a year after final fitting. Additionally, patients come back for follow-up visits to make sure the prosthesis or orthosis has no wear and tear, is working properly, and is in optimal condition.

To become a prosthetist or orthotist, you must complete a four-year undergraduate degree, plus a master's in orthotics and prosthetics.

Beginning in January 2013, the National Commission on Orthotics and Prosthetics Education (NCOPE) ruled that a master's degree in orthotics or prosthetics is the minimum educational standard to become a certified practitioner. Prior to this, all the education needed to be a working orthotist or prosthetist was a four-year bachelor's degree and an additional certification.

Master's degree programs usually take two years to complete: One year is dedicated to classroom learning and one year is spent in a residency program, focusing on hands-on training in different prosthetic/orthotic clinics and practices. The average salary for a prosthetist or orthotist is $64,000 a year and the field has a 1.6 percent unemployment rate.

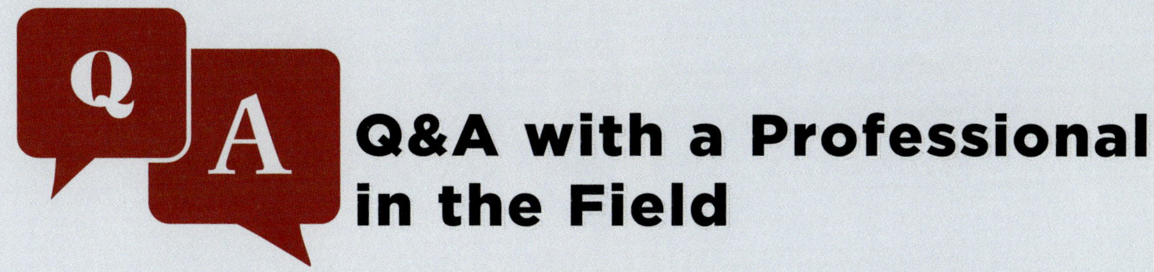

Q&A with a Professional in the Field

What follows is the transcript of an interview with Frank Coffey, a prosthetist working in the field today. Frank discussed his career and how he thinks the profession will change over the next decade.

Question: How long have you been a prosthetist?

Frank: Five years.

Question: What is your specialty and why did you choose it?

Frank: We do not really have specialties. Over time you can get a type of acknowledgment of experience from the certifying body, whether it be for upper extremity or lower extremity. But a real specialized training on a specific upper extremity or lower extremity does not really happen. When you learn, you kind of learn it all, and the practice where you work also affects the exposure you get to certain patients.

Question: Are there any specific practices people go into?

Frank: Well, the type of practice I am in is a prosthetics-only practice, so that means we specialize in prosthetics and that is the only thing we do. So we have a three-dimensional printer and scanner, and we are constantly trying to develop new adaptive equipment and new adaptive designs. This as opposed to some *"turn and burn" practices* that have a steady influx of people and it is all really a numbers game for them. They are just trying to get people in and out the door. We are specialized in the sense that we are an out-of-network provider, as opposed to being in-network. So it allows us to invest more in our patients as a result of that.

Question: What has been the most challenging aspect of your job?

Frank: One of the most challenging aspects, for us, is getting the payers—namely, insurance companies—to acknowledge and respect the use of technology in the elderly population. While technology is continually pushing ahead, more and more baby boomers are coming into the elderly population and we are met with the challenge in working with the payer system to advocate for these patients, getting them the most advanced options in the market. Additionally, it is certainly challenging for myself when it comes to looking at the development of technology. It is a constant challenge to stay on top of developments in the field, as well as looking ahead to products that are in a trial phase. While this is challenging, I know that technology is the true future for my job and where the continued job growth will be. Those who understand what products are available, and how those prostheses can be best selected for the particular patient, will be met with the greatest opportunity in the prosthetics field.

Question: What is the most rewarding aspect of your job?

Frank: Getting someone back to functioning for the first time since their amputation is pretty amazing. It is great to know that I worked in getting someone back to their full potential. At one point the person cannot walk and the next day they could be walking, and to know that I played a part in that gives me so much joy. I truly love my job and the patients I help.

Question: What kind of personal traits do you think are important for a prosthetist to have?

Frank: Compassion is definitely a big one, and a strong drive to make things better. Trying to constantly improve, always looking for something better, always trying to come up with new designs and trying to just help people. Technology and medicine are always evolving and moving forward. This means that my field is always changing. I not only have to keep up with new technology, but with new diseases, and movements in biotechnology. So you also have to be very open to different things and very adaptable.

Question: Prosthetists' shifts are much different from those in the corporate world. Can you please explain the kinds of shifts a prosthetist is expected to work, and talk a little about the toll these can take on your body, mind, and health as a whole?

Frank: Yeah, you are on call, within reason; it is a more than a nine-to-five type of thing. Things sometimes break, and usually it is not at the best time, like right before a holiday. But sometimes I have to come in to make repairs, and make sure the prosthesis is still functional. Because, if not, the person is not walking and that means they are not at their potential so you have to be able to accommodate for their needs at any time of the day or any time of the year.

Question: Who do you look up to in your profession and why?

Frank: Probably everyone before me, the people I trained under. The people who showed me to not just keep doing the same thing, and to try to keep improving and to try to push the envelope prosthetically and even in insurance, so people are able to obtain these devices.

Question: What kind of technology do you use each day?

Frank: A 3-D printer, software programs for the designing, definitely my hands. I use plaster modification, so I do not use a CAD program, which is computer-aided design, where people just make the prosthesis through computer programming. I use a software processor for particular needs, but definitely my hands. I still do a manual removal, for the models, the limb models, and regular bench tools.

Question: Is this job what you expected when you first made the decision to get into this field?

Frank: No. With the insurance payers, I did not realize how much effort it would take to make sure that the patients receive the appropriate prosthetic design. Going into the job, I thought it would be easier, not really such a big issue

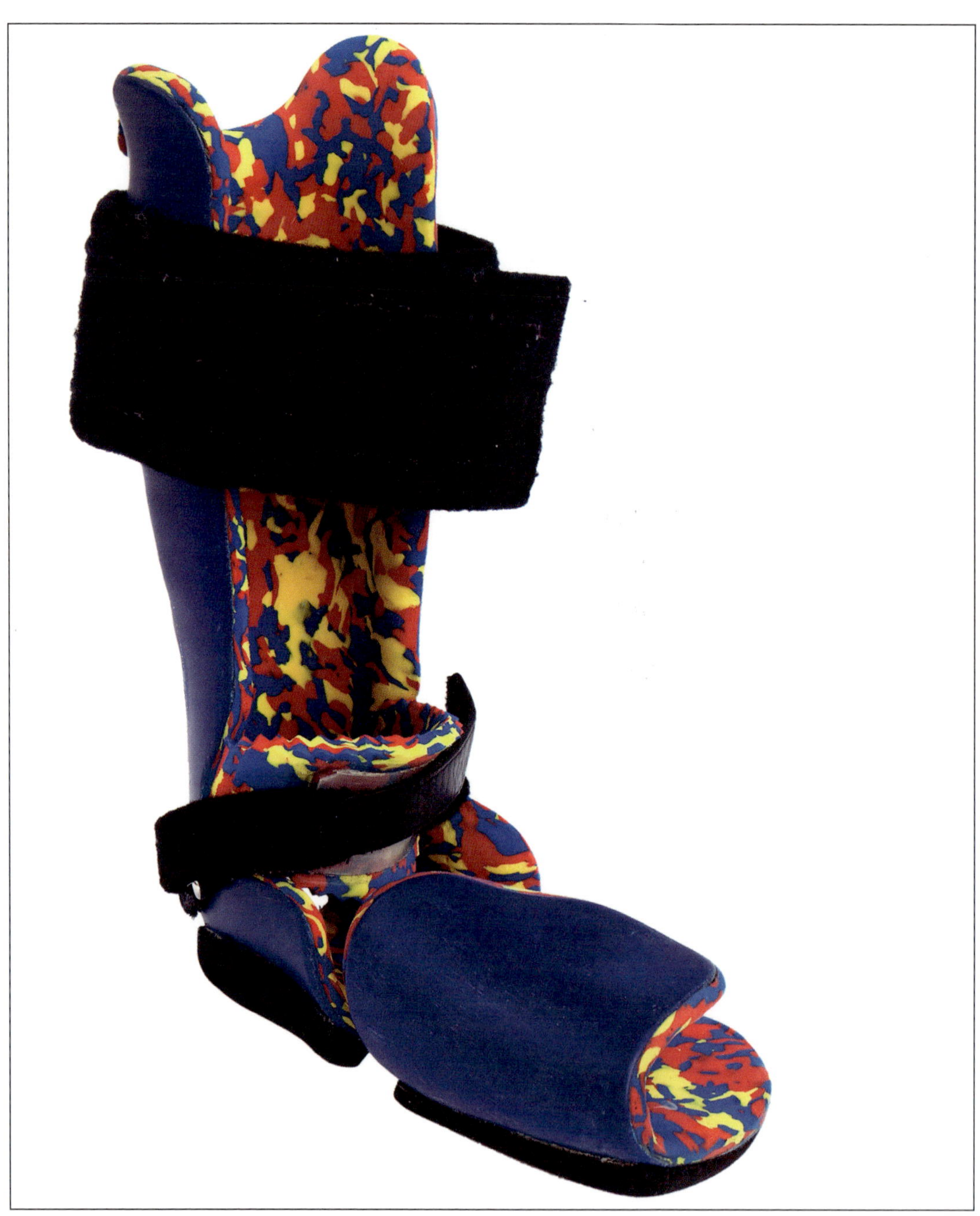

An orthopedic brace like this can help to correct club foot in children.

with insurance companies to pay for these prostheses. But it is a constant challenge I face every day. Some patients cannot afford these machines and we really have to make sure to accommodate or try to get them on payment plans, because in the long run we want any patient who comes through our door to get help and to hopefully get to their full potential.

Question: In your mind, what makes for a successful prosthetist?

Frank: Definitely compassion, and hard work. You need to think about things, even after hours, to make sure patients have everything at their disposal. You have to be extremely compassionate and able to feel for the patients. As a prosthetist, you have to be extremely understanding of the patient, and the patient's struggles. It is extremely difficult to lose a limb and you have to be fully there for these patients.

Question: Can you take me through the step-by-step process someone goes through to get a prosthesis?

Frank: From day one, you will make an initial evaluation, where you evaluate the entire person, and not just the limb. You are trying to figure out what they liked to do prior to the amputation; that is, what they were doing prior to the amputation. You figure out the goals and everything else. Then, from there, you start to figure out the actual prosthetic design that will help them be able to reach those goals and carry out those activities. Once you have a preliminary design, you work with the patient to come up with it. You then take plasters and take impressions or casts of the limb. And once you have the cast of the limb, you basically fill it with dental plaster and then modify the master model plaster down to make the socket. Then you fabricate a test socket, fit the test socket, and make sure that it is comfortable, functional, and all the alignments are appropriate for whatever components are on there. Also, you check the programming and if it is appropriate for whatever components are on there, any microprocessors on there. Then once the test socket looks good and comfortable, you go to a laminated version of that socket where you have carbon fiber and flexible inners, or silicone inners. It could be a silicon socket or whatever design is indicated by the initial evaluation. We make the final socket so it is durable and functional and should be able to get them back to what they want to do within reason.

Question: What would you say to a young adult considering becoming a prosthetist?

Frank: It is a great career to get into. It's definitely a rewarding field. I would not do anything else. It is something you can definitely make a career out of and really make a huge impact on the people you work with. Also, you can see pretty fast results: Someone can literally roll into your office and walk out the same day. It is pretty amazing. I would recommend this career for anyone who has a strong drive to help people and to be constantly striving for improvement. It is extremely important for people going into this field to understand they have to constantly try to improve, not only the prostheses they create, but the prosthetics field as a whole.

Text-Dependent Questions

1. What is one of the personal traits Frank feels is important to be a successful prosthetist?
2. What advice does Frank give to those considering a career as a prosthetist or orthotist? Why would the ability to study come into play after graduation?

Research Project

Look into programs in your school that offer classes that might be relevant to relevant to the orthotist and prosthetist professions. If possible, take classes in biology, chemistry, human anatomy, or even statistics to prepare for later schooling in a prosthetics or orthotics program.

Series Glossary

accredited—a college or university program that has met all of the requirements put forth by the national organization for that job. The official stamp of approval for a degree.

Allied Health Professions—a group of professionals who use scientific principles to evaluate, diagnose and treat a variety of diseases. They also promote overall wellness and disease prevention in support of a variety of health care settings. (These may include physical therapists, dental hygienists, athletic trainers, audiologists, etc.)

American Medical Association (AMA)—the AMA is a professional group of physicians that publishes research about different areas of medicine. The AMA also advocates for its members to define medical concepts, professions, and recommendations.

anatomy—the study of the structure of living things; a person and/or animal's body.

associate's degree—a degree that is awarded to a student who has completed two years of study at a junior college, college, or university.

bachelor's degree—a degree that is awarded to a student by a college or university, usually after four years of study.

biology—the life processes especially of an organism or group.

chemistry—a science that deals with the composition, structure, and properties of substances and with the transformations that they undergo.

cardiology—the study of the heart and its action and diseases.

cardiopulmonary resuscitation (CPR)—a procedure designed to restore normal breathing after cardiac arrest that includes the clearance of air passages to the lungs, mouth-to-mouth method of artificial respiration, and heart massage by the exertion of pressure on the chest.

Centers for Disease Control—the Centers for Disease Control and Prevention (CDC) is a federal agency that conducts and supports health promotion, prevention and preparedness activities in the United States with the goal of improving overall public health.

diagnosis—to determine what is wrong with a patient. This process is especially important because it will determine the type of treatment the patient receives.

diagnostic testing—any tests performed to help determine a medical diagnosis.

EKG machine—an electrocardiogram (EKG or ECG) is a test that checks for problems with the electrical activity of your heart. An EKG shows the heart's electrical activity as line tracings on paper. The spikes and dips in the tracings are called waves. The heart is a muscular pump made up of four chambers.

first responder—the initial personnel who rush to the scene of an accident or an emergency.

Health Insurance Portability and Accountability Act (HIPAA)—a federal law enacted in 1996 that protects continuity of health coverage when a person changes or loses a job, that limits health-plan exclusions for preexisting medical conditions, that requires that patient medical information be kept private and secure, that standardizes electronic transactions involving health information, and that permits tax deduction of health insurance premiums by the self-employed.

internship—the position of a student or trainee who works in an organization, sometimes without pay, in order to gain work experience or satisfy requirements for a qualification.

kinesiology—the study of the principles of mechanics and anatomy in relation to human movement.

Master of Science degree—a Master of Science is a master's degree in the field of science awarded by universities in many countries, or a person holding such a degree.

obesity—a condition characterized by the excessive accumulation and storage of fat in the body.

pediatrics—the branch of medicine dealing with children.

physiology—a branch of biology that deals with the functions and activities of life or of living matter (as organs, tissues, or cells) and of the physical and chemical phenomena involved.

Surgeon General—the operational head of the US Public Health Department and the leading spokesperson for matters of public health.

Further Reading

Barry, Max. *Machine Man*. New York: Vintage Contemporaries, 2011.

Hasegawa, Guy R. *Mending Broken Soldiers: The Union and Confederate Programs to Supply Artificial Limbs.* Carbondale, Ill.: Southern Illinois University Press, 2012.

Ott, Katherine, David Serlin, and Stephen Mihm, eds. *Artificial Parts, Practical Lives: Modern Histories of Prosthetics*. New York: New York University Press, 2002.

Internet Resources

www.bls.gov/ooh/healthcare/orthotists-and-prosthetists.htm

This government website provides information on salaries and job outlook for prosthetists and orthotists.

www.oandp.org

The website of the American Academy of Orthotists and Prosthetists provides information about the profession.

http://resident.ncope.org/prostudents/schools

The National Commission on Orthotic and Prosthetic Education provides information on schools that provide degrees or certification in the field.

http://www.opcareers.org

This website provides information on careers in orthotics and prosthetics.

Publisher's Note: The websites listed on this page were active at the time of publication. The publisher is not responsible for websites that have changed their address or discontinued operation since the date of publication. The publisher reviews and updates the websites each time the book is reprinted.

Index

Numbers in ***bold italic*** refer to captions.

About the Author

Samantha Simon has spent her career in healthcare: shadowing medical professionals, working in medical research, and as a patient liaison advocate within the industry. Her work authoring and writing about her experiences, and further studies into various aspects of the healthcare profession, has gained her unique insight into various aspects of the careers in the field of healthcare. Samantha received her Bachelor's Degree in Health Sciences Pre- Clinical Studies at the University of Central Florida. She has written and studied extensively in Neurobiology, Microbiology, Physiology, and Epidemiology, as well as worked on Medical Self-Assessment, Health Laws and Ethics, and Research Methods. She enjoys authoring and mentoring and lives in South Florida with her family and friends.

Picture Credits: © Andrei Aristide | Dreamstime.com: 36; © Aspenphoto | Dreamstime.com: 11; © Belahoche | Dreamstime.com: 20, 23, 24, 28; © Ben Bibikov | Dreamstime.com: 42; © Cdonofrio | Dreamstime.com: 32; © Stefano Ember | Dreamstime.com: 12, 22; © Karen Foley | Dreamstime.com: 26; © Kolotype | Dreamstime.com: 14; © Mykola Komarovskyy | Dreamstime.com: 46; © Photographerlondon | Dreamstime.com: 16; © Pixattitude | Dreamstime.com: 44; © Seanyu | Dreamstime.com: 30; © Peter Sobolev | Dreamstime.com: 10; © Stainedglass | Dreamstime.com: 6; Library of Congress: 39, 41; used under license from Shutterstock, Inc.: 1, 2, 49, 53, 54.